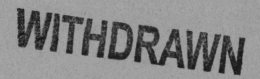

THE
SHIELD
OF
ACHILLES

THE
SHIELD
OF
ACHILLES

W. H. AUDEN

RANDOM HOUSE · NEW YORK

Second Printing

821.91
Au2s

33,602

March, 1956

For Lincoln and Fidelma Kirstein

From bad lands where eggs are small and dear
Climbing to worse by a stonier
Track, when all are spent we hear it—the right song
For the wrong time of year.

Note

I owe my readers an explanation for reprinting two poems, *Prime* and *Nones* which appeared in my previous volume. They were planned to be part of a sequence which is now complete, and it is in their proper context that I would prefer them to be read.

Thanks are due to the following publishers and periodicals in whose pages some of these poems have appeared: *Messrs. Boosey and Hawkes, Ballantine Books, The Times Literary Supplement, The Listener, Encounter, The London Magazine, Botteghe Oscure, Poetry, The Catholic Worker, The Third Hour, The New Yorker, Ariel Poems* (Faber and Faber).

Contents

I

BUCOLICS

Fair is Middle-Earth nor changes, though to Age,
Raging at his uncomeliness,
Her wine turn sour, her bread tasteless.

Winds

(FOR ALEXIS LEGER)

Deep below our violences,
Quite still, lie our First Dad, his watch
    And many little maids,
But the boneless winds that blow
    Round law-court and temple
Recall to Metropolis
    That Pliocene Friday when,
At His holy insufflation
    (Had He picked a teleost
Or an arthropod to inspire,
    Would our death also have come?),
One bubble-brained creature said—
    "I am loved, therefore I am"—:
And well by now might the lion
    Be lying down with the kid,
Had he stuck to that logic.

Winds make weather; weather
Is what nasty people are
    Nasty about and the nice
Show a common joy in observing:
    When I seek an image
For our Authentic City
    (Across what brigs of dread,
Down what gloomy galleries,
    Must we stagger or crawl
Before we may cry—O look!?),
    I see old men in hallways
Tapping their barometers,

Or a lawn over which,
The first thing after breakfast,
    A paterfamilias
Hurries to inspect his rain-gauge.

Goddess of winds and wisdom,
    When, on some windless day
Of dejection, unable
    To name or to structure,
Your poet with bodily tics,
    Scratching, tapping his teeth,
Tugging the lobe of an ear,
    Unconsciously invokes You,
Show Your good nature, allow
    Rooster or whistling maid
To fetch him Arthur O'Bower;
    Then, if moon-faced Nonsense,
That erudite forger, stalk
    Through the seven kingdoms,
Set Your poplars a-shiver
    To warn Your clerk lest he
Die like an Old Believer
    For some spurious reading:
And in all winds, no matter
    Which of Your twelve he may hear,
Equinox gales at midnight
    Howling through marram grass,
Or a faint susurration
    Of pines on a cloudless
Afternoon in midsummer,
    Let him feel You present,

That every verbal rite
   May be fittingly done,
And done in anamnesis
   Of what is excellent
Yet a visible creature,
   Earth, Sky, a few dear names.

Woods

(FOR NICHOLAS NABAKOV)

Sylvan meant savage in those primal woods
Piero di Cosimo so loved to draw,
Where nudes, bears, lions, sows with women's heads
Mounted and murdered and ate each other raw,
Nor thought the lightning-kindled bush to tame
But, flabbergasted, fled the useful flame.

Reduced to patches owned by hunting squires
Of villages with ovens and stocks,
They whispered still of most unsocial fires,
Though Crown and Mitre warned their silly flocks
The pasture's humdrum rhythms to approve
And to abhor the licence of the grove.

Guilty intention still looks for a hotel
That wants no details and surrenders none;
A wood is that, and throws in charm as well,
And many a semi-innocent, undone,
Has blamed its nightingales who round the deed
Sang with such sweetness of a happy greed.

Those birds, of course, did nothing of the sort,
And, as for sylvan nature, if you take
A snapshot at a picnic, O how short
And lower-ordersy the Gang will look
By those vast lives that never took another
And are not scared of gods, ghosts, or stepmother.

Among these coffins of its by-and-by
The Public can (it cannot on a coast)
Bridle its skirt-and-bargain-chasing eye,
And where should an austere philologist
Relax but in the very world of shade
From which the matter of his field was made.

Old sounds re-educate an ear grown coarse,
As Pan's green father suddenly raps out
A burst of undecipherable Morse,
And cuckoos mock in Welsh, and doves create
In rustic English over all they do
To rear their modern family of two.

Now here, now there, some loosened element,
A fruit in vigor or a dying leaf,
Utters its private idiom for descent,
And late man, listening through his latter grief,
Hears, close or far, the oldest of his joys,
Exactly as it was, the water noise.

A well-kempt forest begs Our Lady's grace;
Someone is not disgusted, or at least
Is laying bets upon the human race
Retaining enough decency to last;
The trees encountered on a country stroll
Reveal a lot about that country's soul.

A small grove massacred to the last ash,
An oak with heart-rot, give away the show:
This great society is going smash;
They cannot fool us with how fast they go,
How much they cost each other and the gods!
A culture is no better than its woods.

Mountains

(FOR HEDWIG PETZOLD)

I know a retired dentist who only paints mountains,
    But the Masters seldom care
That much, who sketch them in beyond a holy face
    Or a highly dangerous chair;
  While a normal eye perceives them as a wall
Between worse and better, like a child, scolded in France,
Who wishes he were crying on the Italian side of the Alps:
    Caesar does not rejoice when high ground
      Makes a darker map,
  Nor does Madam. Why should they? A serious being
    Cries out for a gap.

And it is curious how often in steep places
    You meet someone short who frowns,
A type you catch beheading daisies with a stick:
    Small crooks flourish in big towns,
  But perfect monsters—remember Dracula—
Are bred on crags in castles; those unsmiling parties,
Clumping off at dawn in the gear of their mystery
    For points up, are a bit alarming;
    They have the balance, nerve
And habit of the Spiritual, but what God
    Does their Order serve?

A civil man is a citizen. Am I
        To see in the Lake District, then,
Another bourgeois invention like the piano?
        Well, I won't. How can I, when
I wish I stood now on a platform at Penrith,
Zurich, or any junction at which you leave the express
For a local that swerves off soon into a cutting? Soon
        Tunnels begin, red farms disappear,
            Hedges turn to walls,
Cows become sheep, you smell peat or pinewood, you hear
            Your first waterfalls,

And what looked like a wall turns out to be a world
        With measurements of its own
And a style of gossip. To manage the Flesh,
        When angels of ice and stone
Stand over her day and night who make it so plain
They detest any kind of growth, does not encourage
Euphemisms for the effort: here wayside crucifixes
        Bear witness to a physical outrage,
            And serenades too
Stick to bare fact;—"O my girl has a goitre,
            I've a hole in my shoe!"

Dour. Still, a fine refuge. That boy behind his goats
     Has the round skull of a clan
That fled with bronze before a tougher metal.
     And that quiet old gentleman
With a cheap room at the Black Eagle used to own
Three papers but is not received in Society now:
These farms can always see a panting government coming;
     I'm nordic myself, but even so
          I'd much rather stay
Where the nearest person who could have me hung is
     Some ridges away.

To be sitting in privacy, like a cat
     On the warm roof of a loft,
Where the high-spirited son of some gloomy tarn
     Comes sprinting down through a green croft,
Bright with flowers laid out in exquisite splodges
Like a Chinese poem, while, near enough, a real darling
Is cooking a delicious lunch, would keep me happy for
     What? Five minutes? For an uncatlike
          Creature who has gone wrong,
Five minutes on even the nicest mountain
     Is awfully long.

Lakes

(FOR ISAIAH BERLIN)

A lake allows an average father, walking slowly,
　　To circumvent it in an afternoon,
And any healthy mother to halloo the children
　　Back to her bedtime from their games across:
(Anything bigger than that, like Michigan or Baikal,
　　Though potable, is an "estranging sea").

Lake-folk require no fiend to keep them on their toes;
　　They leave aggression to ill-bred romantics
Who duel with their shadows over blasted heaths:
　　A month in a lacustrine atmosphere
Would find the fluvial rivals waltzing not exchanging
　　The rhyming insults of their great-great-uncles.

No wonder Christendom did not get really started
　　Till, scarred by torture, white from caves and jails,
Her pensive chiefs converged on the Ascanian Lake
　　And by that stork-infested shore invented
The life of Godhead, making catholic the figure
　　Of three small fishes in a triangle.

Sly Foreign Ministers should always meet beside one,
　　For, whether they walk widdershins or deasil,
Its path will yoke their shoulders to one liquid centre
　　Like two old donkeys pumping as they plod;
Such physical compassion may not guarantee
　　A marriage for their armies, but it helps.

Only a very wicked or conceited man,
    About to sink somewhere in mid-Atlantic,
Could think Poseidon's frown was meant for him in person,
    But it is only human to believe
The little lady of the glacier lake has fallen
    In love with the rare bather whom she drowns.

The drinking water of the city where one panics
    At nothing noticing how real one is
May come from reservoirs whose guards are all too conscious
    Of being followed: Webster's cardinal
Saw in a fish-pool something horrid with a hay-rake;
    I know a Sussex hammer-pond like that.

A haunted lake is sick, though; normally, they doctor
    Our tactile fevers with a visual world
Where beaks are dumb like boughs and faces safe like houses;
    The water-scorpion finds it quite unticklish,
And, if it shudder slightly when caressed by boats,
    It never asks for water or a loan.

Liking one's Nature, as lake-lovers do, benign
    Goes with a wish for savage dogs and man-traps:
One Fall, one dispossession, is enough, I'm sorry;
    Why should I give Lake Eden to the Nation
Just because every mortal Jack and Jill has been
    The genius of some amniotic mere?

It is unlikely I shall ever keep a swan
    Or build a tower on any small tombolo,
But that's not going to stop me wondering what sort
    Of lake I would decide on if I should.
Moraine, pot, oxbow, glint, sink, crater, piedmont, dimple . . . ?
    Just reeling off their names is ever so comfy.

Islands

(FOR GIOCONDO SACCHETTI)

Old saints on millstones float with cats
    To islands out at sea,
Whereon no female pelvis can
    Threaten their agape.

Beyond the long arm of the Law,
    Close to a shipping road,
Pirates in their island lairs
    Observe the pirate code.

Obsession with security
    In Sovereigns prevails;
His Highness and The People both
    Pick islands for their jails.

Once, where detected worldlings now
    Do penitential jobs,
Exterminated species played
    Who had not read their Hobbes.

His continental damage done,
    Laid on an island shelf,
Napoleon has five years more
    To talk about himself.

How fascinating is that class
    Whose only member is Me!
Sappho, Tiberius and I
    Hold forth beside the sea.

What is cosier than the shore
    Of a lake turned inside out?
How do all these other people
    Dare to be about?

In democratic nudity
    Their sexes lie; except
By age or weight you could not tell
    The keeping from the kept.

They go, she goes, thou goest, I go
    To a mainland livelihood:
Farmer and fisherman complain
    The other has it good.

Plains

(FOR WENDELL JOHNSON)

I can imagine quite easily ending up
　　In a decaying port on a desolate coast,
Cadging drinks from the unwary, a quarrelsome,
　　Disreputable old man; I can picture
A second childhood in a valley, scribbling
　　Reams of edifying and unreadable verse;
But I cannot see a plain without a shudder;—
　　"O God, please, please, don't ever make me live there!"

It's horrible to think what peaks come down to,
　　That pecking rain and squelching glacier defeat
Tall pomps of stone where goddesses lay sleeping,
　　Dreaming of being woken by some chisel's kiss,
That what those blind brutes leave when they are through is nothing
　　But a mere substance, a clay that meekly takes
The potter's cuff, a gravel that as concrete
　　Will unsex any space which it encloses.

And think of growing where all elsewheres are equal!
　　So long as there's a hill-ridge somewhere the dreamer
Can place his land of marvels; in poor valleys
　　Orphans can head downstream to seek a million:
Here nothing points; to choose between Art and Science
　　An embryo genius would have to spin a stick.
What could these farms do if set loose but drift like clouds?
　　What goal of unrest is there but the Navy?

Romance? Not in this weather. Ovid's charmer
    Who leads the quadrilles in Arcady, boy-lord
Of hearts who can call their Yes and No their own,
    Would, madcap that he is, soon die of cold or sunstroke:
These lives are in firmer hands; that old grim She
    Who makes the blind dates for the hatless genera
Creates their country matters. (Woe to the child-bed,
    Woe to the strawberries if She's in Her moods!)

And on these attend, greedy as fowl and harsher
    Than any climate, Caesar with all his They.
If a tax-collector disappear in the hills,
    If, now and then, a keeper is shot in the forest,
No thunder follows, but where roads run level,
    How swift to the point of protest strides the Crown.
It hangs, it flogs, it fines, it goes. There is drink.
    There are wives to beat. But Zeus is with the strong,

Born as a rule in some small place (an island,
    Quite often, where a smart lad can spot the bluff
Whence cannon would put the harbor at his mercy),
    But it's here they chamber with Clio. At this brook
The Christian cross-bow stopped the Heathen scimitar;
    Here is a windmill whence an emperor saw
His right wing crumple; across these cabbage fields
    A pretender's Light Horse made their final charge.

If I were a plainsman I should hate us all,
    From the mechanic rioting for a cheap loaf
To the fastidious palate, hate the painter
    Who steals my wrinkles for his Twelve Apostles,
Hate the priest who cannot even make it shower.
    What could I smile at as I trudged behind my harrow
But bloodshot images of rivers screaming,
    Marbles in panic, and Don't-Care made to care?

As it is, though, I know them personally
    Only as a landscape common to two nightmares:
Across them, spotted by spiders from afar,
    I have tried to run, knowing there was no hiding and no help;
On them, in brilliant moonlight, I have lost my way
    And stood without a shadow at the dead centre
Of an abominable desolation,
    Like Tarquin ravished by his post-coital sadness.

Which goes to show I've reason to be frightened
    Not of plains, of course, but of me. I should like
—Who wouldn't?—to shoot beautifully and be obeyed
    (I should also like to own a cave with two exits);
I wish I weren't so silly. Though I can't pretend
    To think these flats poetic, it's as well at times
To be reminded that nothing is lovely,
    Not even in poetry, which is not the case.

27

Streams

(FOR ELIZABETH DREW)

Dear water, clear water, playful in all your streams,
As you dash or loiter through life who does not love
　　　To sit beside you, to hear you and see you,
　　Pure being, perfect in music and movement?

Air is boastful at times, earth slovenly, fire rude,
But you in your bearing are always immaculate,
　　　The most well-spoken of all the older
　　Servants in the household of Mrs. Nature.

Nobody suspects you of mocking him, for you still
Use the same vocables you were using the day
　　　Before that unexpected row which
　　Downed every hod on half-finished Babel,

And still talk to yourself: nowhere are you disliked;
Arching your torso, you dive from a basalt sill,
　　　Canter across white chalk, slog forward
　　Through red marls, the aboriginal pilgrim,

At home in all sections, but for whom we should be
Idolaters of a single rock, kept apart
　　　By our landscapes, excluding as alien
　　The tales and diets of all other strata.

How could we love the absent one if you did not keep
Coming from a distance, or quite directly assist,
  As when past Iseult's tower you floated
  The willow pash-notes of wanted Tristram?

And *Homo Ludens*, surely, is your child, who make
Fun of our feuds by opposing identical banks,
  Transferring the loam from Huppim
  To Muppim and back each time you crankle.

Growth cannot add to your song: as unchristened brooks
Already you whisper to ants what, as Brahma's son,
  Descending his titanic staircase
  Into Assam, to Himalayan bears you thunder.

And not even man can spoil you: his company
Coarsens roses and dogs but, should he herd you through a sluice
  To toil at a turbine, or keep you
  Leaping in gardens for his amusement,

Innocent still is your outcry, water, and there
Even, to his soiled heart raging at what it is,
  Tells of a sort of world, quite other,
  Altogether different from this one

With its envies and passports, a polis like that
To which, in the name of scholars everywhere,
  Gaston Paris pledged his allegiance
  As Bismarck's siege-guns came within earshot.

Lately, in that dale of all Yorkshire's the loveliest,
Where, off its fell-side helter-skelter, Kisdon Beck
      Jumps into Swale with a boyish shouting,
    Sprawled out on grass, I dozed for a second,

And found myself following a croquet tournament
In a calm enclosure with thrushes popular:
      Of all the players in that cool valley
    The best with the mallet was my darling.

While, on the wolds that begirdled it, wild old men
Hunted with spades and hammers, monomaniac each,
      For a megalith or a fossil,
    And bird-watchers stalked the mossy beech-woods.

Suddenly, over the lawn we started to run
For, lo, through the trees in a cream and golden coach
      Drawn by two baby locomotives,
    The god of mortal doting approached us,

Flanked by his bodyguard, those hairy armigers in green
Who laugh at thunderstorms and weep at a blue sky:
      He thanked us for our cheers of homage,
    And promised X and Y a passion undying.

With a wave of his torch he commanded a dance;
So round in a ring we flew, my dear on my right,
      When I awoke. But fortunate seemed that
    Day because of my dream and enlightened,

And dearer, water, than ever your voice, as if
Glad—though goodness knows why—to run with the human race,
   Wishing, I thought, the least of men their
   Figures of splendor, their holy places.

IN SUNSHINE AND IN SHADE

Guard, Civility, with guns
Your modes and your declensions;
Any lout can spear with ease
Singular Archimedes.

The Shield of Achilles

    She looked over his shoulder
        For vines and olive trees,
    Marble well-governed cities,
        And ships upon untamed seas,
    But there on the shining metal
        His hands had put instead
    An artificial wilderness
        And a sky like lead.

A plain without a feature, bare and brown,
    No blade of grass, no sign of neighborhood,
Nothing to eat and nowhere to sit down,
    Yet, congregated on its blankness, stood
    An unintelligible multitude.
A million eyes, a million boots in line,
Without expression, waiting for a sign.

Out of the air a voice without a face
    Proved by statistics that some cause was just
In tones as dry and level as the place:
    No one was cheered and nothing was discussed;
    Column by column in a cloud of dust
They marched away enduring a belief
Whose logic brought them, somewhere else, to grief.

She looked over his shoulder
    For ritual pieties,
White flower-garlanded heifers,
    Libation and sacrifice,
But there on the shining metal
    Where the altar should have been,
She saw by his flickering forge-light
    Quite another scene.

Barbed wire enclosed an arbitrary spot
    Where bored officials lounged (one cracked a joke)
And sentries sweated, for the day was hot:
    A crowd of ordinary decent folk
    Watched from without and neither moved nor spoke
As three pale figures were led forth and bound
To three posts driven upright in the ground.

The mass and majesty of this world, all
    That carries weight and always weighs the same,
Lay in the hands of others; they were small
    And could not hope for help and no help came:
    What their foes liked to do was done, their shame
Was all the worst could wish; they lost their pride
And died as men before their bodies died.

She looked over his shoulder
    For athletes at their games,
Men and women in a dance
    Moving their sweet limbs
Quick, quick, to music,
    But there on the shining shield
His hands had set no dancing-floor
    But a weed-choked field.

A ragged urchin, aimless and alone,
    Loitered about that vacancy; a bird
Flew up to safety from his well-aimed stone:
    That girls are raped, that two boys knife a third,
    Were axioms to him, who'd never heard
Of any world where promises were kept
Or one could weep because another wept.

    The thin-lipped armorer,
        Hephaestos, hobbled away;
    Thetis of the shining breasts
        Cried out in dismay
    At what the god had wrought
        To please her son, the strong
    Iron-hearted man-slaying Achilles
        Who would not live long.

Fleet Visit

The sailors come ashore
Out of their hollow ships,
Mild-looking middle-class boys
Who read the comic strips;
One baseball game is more
To them than fifty Troys.

They look a bit lost, set down
In this unamerican place
Where natives pass with laws
And futures of their own;
They are not here because
But only just-in-case.

The whore and ne'er-do-well
Who pester them with junk
In their grubby ways at least
Are serving the Social Beast;
They neither make nor sell—
No wonder they get drunk.

But the ships on the dazzling blue
Of the harbor actually gain
From having nothing to do;
Without a human will
To tell them whom to kill
Their structures are humane

And, far from looking lost,
Look as if they were meant
To be pure abstract design
By some master of pattern and line,
Certainly worth every cent
Of the millions they must have cost.

Hunting Season

A shot: from crag to crag
    The tell-tale echoes trundle;
Some feathered he-or-she
    Is now a lifeless bundle
And, proud into a kitchen, some
Example of our tribe will come.

Down in the startled valley
    Two lovers break apart:
He hears the roaring oven
    Of a witch's heart;
Behind his murmurs of her name
She sees a marksman taking aim.

Reminded of the hour
    And that his chair is hard,
A deathless verse half done,
    One interrupted bard
Postpones his dying with a dish
Of several suffocated fish.

The Willow-Wren and the Stare

A starling and a willow-wren,
    On a may-tree by a weir,
Saw them meet and heard him say;
    "Dearest of my dear,
More lively than these waters chortling
    As they leap the dam,
My sweetest duck, my precious goose,
    My white lascivious lamb."
With a smile she listened to him;
    Talking to her there:
What does he want? said the willow-wren;
    Much too much, said the stare.

"Forgive these loves who dwell in me,
    These brats of greed and fear,
The honking bottom-pinching clown,
    The snivelling sonneteer,
That so, between us, even these,
    Who till the grave are mine,
For all they fall so short of may,
    Dear heart, be still a sign."
With a smile she closed her eyes,
    Silent she lay there:
Does he mean what he says? said the willow-wren;
    Some of it, said the stare.

"Hark! Wild Robin winds his horn
    And, as his notes require,
Now our laughter-loving spirits
    Must in awe retire
And let their kinder partners,
    Speechless with desire,
Go in their holy selfishness,
    Unfunny to the fire."
Smiling, silently she threw
    Her arms about him there:
Is it only that? said the willow-wren;
    It's that as well, said the stare.

Waking in her arms he cried,
    Utterly content;
"I have heard the high good noises,
    Promoted for an instant,
Stood upon the shining outskirts
    Of that Joy I thank
For you, my dog and every goody."
    There on the grass bank
She laughed, he laughed, they laughed together,
    Then they ate and drank:
Did he know what he meant? said the willow-wren
    God only knows, said the stare.

The Proof

"When rites and melodies begin
    To alter modes and times,
And timid bar-flies boast aloud
    Of uncommitted crimes,
And leading families are proud
    To dine with their black sheep,
What promises, what discipline,
    If any, will Love keep?"
        So roared Fire on their right:
          But Tamino and Pamina
          Walked past its rage,
      Sighing O, sighing O,
In timeless fermatas of awe and delight
      (Innocent? Yes. Ignorant? No.)
        Down the grim passage.

"When stinking Chaos lifts the latch,
    And Grotte backward spins,
And Helen's nose becomes a beak,
    And cats and dogs grow chins,
And daisies claw and pebbles shriek,
    And Form and Color part,
What swarming hatreds then will hatch
    Out of Love's riven heart."
        So hissed Water on their left:
          But Pamina and Tamino
          Opposed its spite,
      With his worship, with her sweetness—
O look now! See how they emerge from the cleft
      (Frightened? No. Happy? Yes.)
        Out into sunlight.

"The Truest Poetry Is the Most Feigning"

(FOR EDGAR WIND)

By all means sing of love but, if you do,
Please make a rare old proper hullabaloo:
When ladies ask *How much do you love me?*
The Christian answer is *così-così*.
But poets are not celibate divines;
Had Dante said so, who would read his lines?
Be subtle, various, ornamental, clever,
And do not listen to those critics ever
Whose crude provincial gullets crave in books
Plain cooking made still plainer by plain cooks,
As though the Muse preferred her half-wit sons;
Good poets have a weakness for bad puns.

Suppose your Beatrice be, as usual, late,
And you would tell us how it feels to wait,
You're free to think, what may be even true,
You're so in love that one hour seems like two,
But write—*As I sat waiting for her call,*
Each second longer darker seemed than all
(Something like this but more elaborate still)
Those raining centuries it took to fill
That quarry whence Endymion's love was torn;
From such ingenious fibs are poems born:
Then, should she leave you for some other guy,
Or ruin you with debts, or go and die,
No metaphor, remember, can express
A real historical unhappiness;
Your tears have value if they make us gay;
O Happy Grief! is all sad verse can say.

The living girl's your business (some odd sorts
Have been an inspiration to men's thoughts):
Yours may be old enough to be your mother,
Or have one leg that's shorter than the other,
Or play Lacrosse or do the Modern Dance;
To you that's destiny, to us it's chance;
We cannot love your love till she take on,
Through you, the wonders of a paragon.
Sing her triumphant passage to our land,
The sun her footstool, the moon in her right hand,
And seven planets blazing in her hair,
Queen of the Night and Empress of the Air;
Tell how her fleet by nine king swans is led,
Wild geese write magic letters overhead
And hippocampi follow in her wake
With Amphisbaene, gentle for her sake;
Sing her descent on the exulting shore
To bless the vines and put an end to war.

If half-way through such praises of your dear,
Riot and shooting fill the streets with fear,
And overnight, as in some terror dream,
Poets are suspect with the New Regime,
Stick at your desk and hold your panic in;
What you are writing may still save your skin:
Re-sex the pronouns, add a few details,
And, lo, a panegyric ode which hails
(How is the Censor, bless his heart, to know?)
The new pot-bellied Generalissimo.
Some epithets, of course, like *lily-breasted*
Need modifying to, say, *lion-chested*,

A title *Goddess of wry-necks and wrens*
To *Great Reticulator of the fens,*
But in an hour your poem qualifies
For a State pension or His annual prize,
And you will die in bed (which He will not:
That silly sausage will be hanged or shot).
Though honest Iagos, true to form, will write
Shame! in your margins, *Toady! Hypocrite!,*
True hearts, clear heads will hear the note of glory
And put inverted commas round the story,
Thinking—*Old Sly-boots! We shall never know
Her name or nature. Well, it's better so.*

For, given Man, by birth, by education,
Imago Dei who forgot his station,
The self-made creature who himself unmakes,
The only creature ever made who fakes,
With no more nature in his loving smile
Than in his theories of a natural style,
What but tall tales, the luck of verbal playing,
Can trick his lying nature into saying
That love, or truth in any serious sense,
Like orthodoxy, is a reticence.

A Sanguine Thought

O where would those choleric boys,
Our political orators, be,
Were one to deprive them of all
Their igneous figures of speech;
If, instead of stamping out flames
Or consuming stubble with fire,
They could only shut out the draught
Or let in a little fresh air?

A Permanent Way

Self-drivers may curse their luck,
Stuck on new-fangled trails,
But the good old train will jog
To the dogma of its rails

And steam so straight ahead
That I cannot be led astray
By tempting scenes which occur
Along any permanent way.

Intriguing dales escape
Into hills of the shape I like,
Though, were I actually put
Where a foot-path leaves the pike

For some steep romantic spot,
I should ask what chance there is
Of at least a ten-dollar cheque
Or a family peck of a kiss:

But, forcibly held to my tracks,
I can safely relax and dream
Of a love and a livelihood
To fit that wood or stream;

And what could be greater fun,
Once one has chosen and paid,
Than the inexpensive delight
Of a choice one might have made.

Barcarolle

(ARIA FROM *The Rake's Progress*)

Gently, little boat,
Across the waters float,
Their crystal waves dividing;
   The sun in the west
   Is going to rest:
      Glide, glide, glide,
Towards the Islands of the Blest.

Orchards greenly grace
That undisturbèd place,
The wearied soul recalling
   To slumber and dream,
   While many a stream
      Falls, falls, falls,
Descanting on a child-like theme.

Lion, lamb and deer,
Untouched by greed or fear,
About its woods are straying,
   And quietly now
   The blossoming bough
      Sways, sways, sways
Above the clear unclouded brow.

Nocturne I

Appearing unannounced, the moon
Avoids a mountain's jagged prongs
And sweeps into the open sky
Like one who knows where she belongs.

To me, immediately, my heart:
"Adore Her, Mother, Virgin, Muse,
A Face worth watching Who can make
Or break you as Her fancy choose."

At which the reflex of my mind:
"You will not tell me, I presume,
That bunch of barren craters care
Who sleeps with or who tortures whom."

Tonight, like umpteen other nights,
The baser frankness wins of course,
My tougher mind which dares admit
That both are worshippers of force.

Granted what both of them believe,
The Goddess, clearly, has to go,
Whose majesty is but the mask
That hides a faceless dynamo;

And neither of my natures can
Complain if I should be reduced
To a small functionary whose dreams
Are vast, unscrupulous, confused.

Supposing, though, my face is real
And not a myth or a machine,
The moon should look like x and wear
Features I've actually seen,

My neighbor's face, a face as such,
Neither a status nor a sex,
Constant for me no matter what
The value I assign to x;

That gushing lady, possibly,
Who brought some verses of her own,
That hang-dog who keeps coming back
For just a temporary loan;

A counter-image, anyway,
To balance with its lack of weight
My world, the private motor-car
And all the engines of the State.

Nocturne II

Make this night lovable,
Moon, and with eye single
Looking down from up there,
Bless me, One especial
And friends everywhere.

With a cloudless brightness
Surround our absences;
Innocent be our sleeps,
Watched by great still spaces,
White hills, glittering deeps.

Parted by circumstance,
Grant each your indulgence
That we may meet in dreams
For talk, for dalliance,
By warm hearths, by cool streams.

Shine lest tonight any,
In the dark suddenly,
Wake alone in a bed
To hear his own fury
Wishing his love were dead.

In Memoriam L. K-A.

At peace under this mandarin, sleep, Lucina,
Blue-eyed Queen of white cats: for you the Ischian wave shall weep,
When we who now miss you are American dust, and steep
Epomeo in peace and war augustly a grave-watch keep.

Epitaph for the Unknown Soldier

To save your world you asked this man to die:
Would this man, could he see you now, ask why?

Ode to Gaea

From this new culture of the air we finally see,
Far-shining in excellence, what our Mother, the
      Nicest daughter of Chaos, would
      Admire could she look in a glass,

And what, in her eyes, is natural: it is the old
Grand style of gesture we watch as, heavy with cold,
      The top-waters of all her
      Northern seas take their vernal plunge,

And suddenly her desolations, salt as blood,
Prolix yet terse, are glamorously carpeted
      With great swatches of plankton,
      Delicious spreads of nourishment,

While, in her realm of solids, lively dots expand,
Companionship becomes an unstaid passion and
      Leaves by the mile hide tons of
      Pied pebbles that will soon be birds.

Now that we know how she looks, she seems more mysterious
Than when, in her *partibus infidelibus*,
      We painted sizzling dragons
      And wizards reading upside down,

But less approachable: where she joins girl's-ear lakes
To bird's-foot deltas with lead-blue squiggles she makes,
      Surely, a value judgment,
      "Of pure things Water is the best,"

But how does she rank wheelwrights? One doubts if she knows
Which sub-species of folly is peculiar to those
        Pretty molehills, where on that
        Pocket-handkerchief of a plain

The syntax changes: peering down sleepily at
A crenelated shore, the tired old diplomat
        Becomes embarrassed—should he
        Smile for "our great good ally," scowl

At "that vast and detestable empire" or choose
The sneer reserved for certain Southern countries "whose
        Status and moral climate
        We have no desire, sir, to emulate?"

But why we should feel neglected on mountain drives,
Unpopular in woods, is quite clear; the older lives
        Have no wish to be stood in
        Rows or at right angles: below,

Straight as its railroads, cutting diagonally across
A positivist republic, two lines of moss
        Show where the Devil's Causeway
        Drew pilgrims seven gods ago,

And, on this eve of whispers and tapped telephones
Before the Ninth Catastrophe, square cornerstones
        Still distinguish a fortress
        Of the High Kings from untutored rock.

Tempting to mortals is the fancy of half-concerned
Gods in the sky, of a bored Thunderer who turned
From the Troy-centred grief to
Watch the Hippemolgoi drink their milk,

And how plausible from his look-point: we may well
Shake a weak fist one day at this vision, but the spell
Of high places will haunt us
Long after our jaunt has declined,

As soon it must, to the hard ground. Where six foot is tall,
Good-manners will ask easy riddles like "Why are all
The rowdiest marches and the
Most venemous iambics composed

By lame clergymen?", will tell no tales which end in worse
Disaster than that of the tipsy poet who cursed
A baby for whom later
He came to sigh—so we were taught

Before the Greater Engines came and the police
Who go with them, when the long rivers ran through peace
And the holy laws of Speech were
Held in awe, even by evil tongues,

And manners, maybe, will stand us in better stead,
Down there, than a kantian conscience: from overhead
Much harm is discernible,
Farms unroofed and harbor-works wrecked

In the Second Assault; frank to an ungrieving sky
As still they look, too many fertilities lie
  In dread of the tormentor's
  Fondling finger, and in the few

That still have poky shops and audiences of one,
Many are overweight, the pious peasant's only son,
  Goading their crumpled faces
  Down innocence-corrupting roads,

Dreams of cities where his cows are whores. When the wise
Wilt in the glare of the Shadow, the stern advise
  Tribute and the large-hearted
  Already talk Its gibberish,

Perhaps a last stand in the passes will be made
By those whose Valhalla would be hearing verse by Praed
  Or arias by Rossini
  Between two entrées by Carême.

We hope so. But who on Cupid's Coming would care to bet?
More than one World's Bane has been scotched before this, yet
  Justice during his *Te Deum*
  Slipped away sighing from the hero's pew,

And Earth, till the end, will be herself; she has never been moved
Except by Amphion, and orators have not improved
  Since misled Athens perished
  Upon Sicilian marble: what,

Prime

Simultaneously, as soundlessly,
    Spontaneously, suddenly
As, at the vaunt of the dawn, the kind
    Gates of the body fly open
To its world beyond, the gates of the mind,
    The horn gate and the ivory gate,
Swing to, swing shut, instantaneously
    Quell the nocturnal rummage
Of its rebellious fronde, ill-favored,
    Ill-natured and second-rate,
Disenfranchised, widowed and orphaned
    By an historical mistake:
Recalled from the shades to be a seeing being,
    From absence to be on display,
Without a name or history I wake
    Between my body and the day.

Holy this moment, wholly in the right,
    As, in complete obedience
To the light's laconic outcry, next
    As a sheet, near as a wall,
Out there as a mountain's poise of stone,
    The world is present, about,
And I know that I am, here, not alone
    But with a world, and rejoice
Unvexed, for the will has still to claim
    This adjacent arm as my own,
The memory to name me, resume
    Its routine of praise and blame,

And smiling to me is this instant while
    Still the day is intact, and I
The Adam sinless in our beginning,
    Adam still previous to any act.

I draw breath; that is of course to wish
    No matter what, to be wise,
To be different, to die and the cost,
    No matter how, is Paradise
Lost of course and myself owing a death:
    The eager ridge, the steady sea,
The flat roofs of the fishing village
    Still asleep in its bunny,
Though as fresh and sunny still, are not friends
    But things to hand, this ready flesh
No honest equal but my accomplice now,
    My assassin to be, and my name
Stands for my historical share of care
    For a lying self-made city,
Afraid of our living task, the dying
    Which the coming day will ask.

Terce

After shaking paws with his dog
(Whose bark would tell the world that he is always kind),
    The hangman sets off briskly over the heath;
He does not know yet who will be provided
    To do the high works of Justice with:
Gently closing the door of his wife's bedroom
    (Today she has one of her headaches),
With a sigh the judge descends his marble stair;
    He does not know by what sentence
He will apply on earth the Law that rules the stars:
    And the poet, taking a breather
Round his garden before starting his eclogue,
    Does not know whose Truth he will tell.

    Sprites of hearth and store-room, godlings
Of professional mysteries, the Big Ones
    Who can annihilate a city,
Cannot be bothered with this moment: we are left,
    Each to his secret cult, now each of us
Prays to an image of his image of himself;
    "Let me get through this coming day
Without a dressing down from a superior,
    Being worsted in a repartee,
Or behaving like an ass in front of the girls;
    Let something exciting happen,
Let me find a lucky coin on a sidewalk,
    Let me hear a new funny story."

At this hour we all might be anyone:
It is only our victim who is without a wish,
          Who knows already (that is what
We can never forgive. If he knows the answers,
          Then why are we here, why is there even dust?),
Knows already that, in fact, our prayers are heard,
          That not one of us will slip up,
That the machinery of our world will function
          Without a hitch, that to-day, for once,
There will be no squabbling on Mount Olympus,
          No Chthonian mutters of unrest,
But no other miracle, knows that by sundown
          We shall have had a good Friday.

Sext

1.

You need not see what someone is doing
to know if it is his vocation,

you have only to watch his eyes:
a cook mixing a sauce, a surgeon

making a primary incision,
a clerk completing a bill of lading,

wear the same rapt expression,
forgetting themselves in a function.

How beautiful it is,
that eye-on-the-object look.

To ignore the appetitive goddesses,
to desert the formidable shrines

of Rhea, Aphrodite, Demeter, Diana,
to pray instead to St. Phocas,

St. Barbara, San Saturnino,
or whoever one's patron is,

that one may be worthy of their mystery,
what a prodigious step to have taken.

There should be monuments, there should be odes,
to the nameless heroes who took it first,

to the first flaker of flints
who forgot his dinner,

the first collector of sea-shells
to remain celibate.

Where should we be but for them?
Feral still, un-housetrained, still

wandering through forests without
a consonant to our names,

slaves of Dame Kind, lacking
all notion of a city

and, at this noon, for this death,
there would be no agents.

2.

You need not hear what orders he is giving
to know if someone has authority,

you have only to watch his mouth:
when a besieging general sees

a city wall breached by his troops,
when a bacteriologist

realizes in a flash what was wrong
with his hypothesis, when,

68

from a glance at the jury, the prosecutor
knows the defendant will hang,

their lips and the lines around them
relax, assuming an expression,

not of simple pleasure at getting
their own sweet way but of satisfaction

at being right, an incarnation
of *Fortitudo, Justicia, Nous.*

You may not like them much
(Who does?) but we owe them

basilicas, divas,
dictionaries, pastoral verse,

the courtesies of the city:
without these judicial mouths

(which belong for the most part
to very great scoundrels)

how squalid existence would be,
tethered for life to some hut village,

afraid of the local snake
or the local ford demon,

speaking the local patois
of some three hundred words

(think of the family squabbles and the
poison-pens, think of the inbreeding)

and, at this noon, there would be no authority
to command this death.

3.

Anywhere you like, somewhere
on broad-chested life-giving Earth,

anywhere between her thirstlands
and undrinkable Ocean,

the crowd stands perfectly still,
its eyes (which seem one) and its mouths

(which seem infinitely many)
expressionless, perfectly blank.

The crowd does not see (what everyone sees)
a boxing match, a train wreck,

a battleship being launched,
does not wonder (as everyone wonders)

who will win, what flag she will fly,
how many will be burned alive,

is never distracted
(as everyone is always distracted)

by a barking dog, a smell of fish,
a mosquito on a bald head:

the crowd sees only one thing
(which only the crowd can see),

an epiphany of that
which does whatever is done.

Whatever god a person believes in,
in whatever way he believes

(no two are exactly alike),
as one of the crowd he believes

and only believes in that
in which there is only one way of believing.

Few people accept each other and most
will never do anything properly,

but the crowd rejects no one, joining the crowd
is the only thing all men can do.

Only because of that can we say
all men are our brothers,

superior, because of that,
to the social exoskeletons: When

have they ever ignored their queens,
for one second stopped work

on their provincial cities, to worship
The Prince of this world like us,

at this noon, on this hill,
in the occasion of this dying.

Nones

What we know to be not possible,
  Though time after time foretold
By wild hermits, by shaman and sybil
  Gibbering in their trances,
Or revealed to a child in some chance rhyme
  Like *will* and *kill*, comes to pass
Before we realize it: we are surprised
  At the ease and speed of our deed
And uneasy: It is barely three,
  Mid-afternoon, yet the blood
Of our sacrifice is already
  Dry on the grass; we are not prepared
For silence so sudden and so soon;
  The day is too hot, too bright, too still,
Too ever, the dead remains too nothing.
  What shall we do till nightfall?

The wind has dropped and we have lost our public.
  The faceless many who always
Collect when any world is to be wrecked,
  Blown up, burnt down, cracked open,
Felled, sawn in two, hacked through, torn apart,
  Have all melted away: not one
Of these who in the shade of walls and trees
  Lie sprawled now, calmly sleeping,
Harmless as sheep, can remember why
  He shouted or what about
So loudly in the sunshine this morning;
  All if challenged would reply

—"It was a monster with one red eye,
　　A crowd that saw him die, not I."—
The hangman has gone to wash, the soldiers to eat:
　　We are left alone with our feat.

The Madonna with the green woodpecker,
　　The Madonna of the fig-tree,
The Madonna beside the yellow dam,
　　Turn their kind faces from us
And our projects under construction,
　　Look only in one direction,
Fix their gaze on our completed work:
　　Pile-driver, concrete-mixer,
Crane and pickaxe wait to be used again,
　　But how can we repeat this?
Outliving our act, we stand where we are,
　　As disregarded as some
Discarded artifact of our own,
　　Like torn gloves, rusted kettles,
Abandoned branch-lines, worn lop-sided
　　Grindstones buried in nettles.

This mutilated flesh, our victim,
　　Explains too nakedly, too well,
The spell of the asparagus garden,
　　The aim of our chalk-pit game; stamps,
Birds' eggs are not the same, behind the wonder
　　Of tow-paths and sunken lanes,
Behind the rapture on the spiral stair,
　　We shall always now be aware
Of the deed into which they lead, under

The mock chase and mock capture,
The racing and tussling and splashing,
    The panting and the laughter,
Be listening for the cry and stillness
    To follow after: wherever
The sun shines, brooks run, books are written,
    There will also be this death.

Soon cool tramontana will stir the leaves,
    The shops will re-open at four,
The empty blue bus in the empty pink square
    Fill up and depart: we have time
To misrepresent, excuse, deny,
    Mythify, use this event
While, under a hotel bed, in prison,
    Down wrong turnings, its meaning
Waits for our lives: sooner than we would choose,
    Bread will melt, water will burn,
And the great quell begin, Abaddon
    Set up his triple gallows
At our seven gates, fat Belial make
    Our wives waltz naked; meanwhile
It would be best to go home, if we have a home,
    In any case good to rest.

That our dreaming wills may seem to escape
    This dead calm, wander instead
On knife edges, on black and white squares,
    Across moss, baize, velvet, boards,
Over cracks and hillocks, in mazes
    Of string and penitent cones,

Down granite ramps and damp passages,
    Through gates that will not relatch
And doors marked *Private*, pursued by Moors
    And watched by latent robbers,
To hostile villages at the heads of fjords,
    To dark châteaux where wind sobs
In the pine-trees and telephones ring,
    Inviting trouble, to a room,
Lit by one weak bulb, where our Double sits
    Writing and does not look up.

That, while we are thus away, our own wronged flesh
    May work undisturbed, restoring
The order we try to destroy, the rhythm
    We spoil out of spite: valves close
And open exactly, glands secrete,
    Vessels contract and expand
At the right moment, essential fluids
    Flow to renew exhausted cells,
Not knowing quite what has happened, but awed
    By death like all the creatures
Now watching this spot, like the hawk looking down
    Without blinking, the smug hens
Passing close by in their pecking order,
    The bug whose view is balked by grass,
Or the deer who shyly from afar
    Peer through chinks in the forest.

Vespers

If the hill overlooking our city has always been known as Adam's Grave, only at dusk can you see the recumbent giant, his head turned to the west, his right arm resting for ever on Eve's haunch,

can you learn, from the way he looks up at the scandalous pair, what a citizen really thinks of his citizenship,

just as now you can hear in a drunkard's caterwaul his rebel sorrows crying for a parental discipline, in lustful eyes perceive a disconsolate soul,

scanning with desperation all passing limbs for some vestige of her faceless angel who in that long ago when wishing was a help mounted her once and vanished:

For Sun and Moon supply their conforming masks, but in this hour of civil twilight all must wear their own faces.

And it is now that our two paths cross.

Both simultaneously recognize his Anti-type: that I am an Arcadian, that he is a Utopian.

He notes, with contempt, my Aquarian belly: I note, with alarm, his Scorpion's mouth.

He would like to see me cleaning latrines: I would like to see him removed to some other planet.

Neither speaks. What experience could we possibly share?

Glancing at a lampshade in a store window, I observe it is too hideous for anyone in their senses to buy: He observes it is too expensive for a peasant to buy.

Passing a slum child with rickets, I look the other way: He looks the other way if he passes a chubby one.

I hope our senators will behave like saints, provided they don't reform me: He hopes they will behave like *baritoni cattivi*, and, when lights burn late in the Citadel,

I (who have never seen the inside of a police station) am shocked and think; "Were the city as free as they say, after sundown all her bureaus would be huge black stones.":

He (who has been beaten up several times) is not shocked at all but thinks; "One fine night our boys will be working up there."

You can see, then, why, between my Eden and his New Jerusalem, no treaty is negotiable.

In my Eden a person who dislikes Bellini has the good manners not to get born: In his New Jerusalem a person who dislikes work will be very sorry he was born.

In my Eden we have a few beam-engines, saddle-tank locomotives, overshot waterwheels and other beautiful pieces of obsolete machinery to play with: In his New Jerusalem even chefs will be cucumber-cool machine minders.

In my Eden our only source of public information is gossip: In his New Jerusalem there will be a special daily in simplified spelling for non-verbal types.

In my Eden each observes his compulsive rituals and superstitious tabus but we have no morals: In his New Jerusalem the temples will be empty but all will practice the rational virtues.

One reason for his contempt is that I have only to close my eyes, cross the iron footbridge to the tow-path, take the barge through the short brick tunnel and

there I stand in Eden again, welcomed back by the krum-horns, doppions, sordumes of jolly miners and a bob major from the Cathedral (romanesque) of St. Sophie (*Die Kalte*):

One reason for my alarm is that, when he closes his eyes, he arrives, not in New Jerusalem, but on some august day of outrage when hellikins cavort through ruined drawing-rooms and fish-wives intervene in the Chamber or

some autumn night of delations and noyades when the unrepentant thieves (including me) are sequestered and those he hates shall hate themselves instead.

So with a passing glance we take the other's posture: Already our steps recede, heading, incorrigible each, towards his kind of meal and evening.

Was it (as it must look to any god of cross-roads) simply a fortuitous intersection of life-paths, loyal to different fibs,

or also a rendezvous between accomplices who, in spite of themselves, cannot resist meeting

to remind the other (do both, at bottom, desire truth?) of that half of their secret which he would most like to forget, forcing us both, for a fraction of a second, to remember our victim (but for him I could forget the blood, but for me he could forget the innocence)

on whose immolation (call him Abel, Remus, whom you will, it is one Sin Offering) arcadias, utopias, our dear old bag of a democracy, are alike founded:

For without a cement of blood (it must be human, it must be innocent) no secular wall will safely stand.

Compline

Now, as desire and the things desired
    Cease to require attention,
As, seizing its chance, the body escapes,
    Section by section, to join
Plants in their chaster peace which is more
    To its real taste, now a day is its past,
Its last deed and feeling in, should come
    The instant of recollection
When the whole thing makes sense: it comes, but all
    I recall are doors banging,
Two housewives scolding, an old man gobbling,
    A child's wild look of envy,
Actions, words, that could fit any tale,
    And I fail to see either plot
Or meaning; I cannot remember
    A thing between noon and three.

Nothing is with me now but a sound,
    A heart's rhythm, a sense of stars
Leisurely walking around, and both
    Talk a language of motion
I can measure but not read: maybe
    My heart is confessing her part
In what happened to us from noon to three,
    That constellations indeed
Sing of some hilarity beyond
    All liking and happening,
But, knowing I neither know what they know
    Nor what I ought to know, scorning

All vain fornications of fancy,
    Now let me, blessing them both
For the sweetness of their cassations,
    Accept our separations.

A stride from now will take me into dream,
    Leave me, without a status,
Among its unwashed tribes of wishes
    Who have no dances and no jokes
But a magic cult to propitiate
    What happens from noon till three,
Odd rites which they hide from me—should I chance,
    Say, on youths in an oak-wood
Insulting a white deer, bribes nor threats
    Will get them to blab—and then
Past untruth is one step to nothing,
    For the end, for me as for cities,
Is total absence: what comes to be
    Must go back into non-being
For the sake of the equity, the rhythm
    Past measure or comprehending.

Can poets (can men in television)
    Be saved? It is not easy
To believe in unknowable justice
    Or pray in the name of a love
Whose name one's forgotten: *libera*
    Me, libera C (dear C)
And all poor s-o-b's who never
    Do anything properly, spare
Us in the youngest day when all are

Shaken awake, facts are facts
(And I shall know exactly
    What happened today between noon and three),
That we, too, may come to the picnic
    With nothing to hide, join the dance
As it moves in perichoresis,
    Turns about the abiding tree.

Lauds

Among the leaves the small birds sing;
The crow of the cock commands awaking:
In solitude, for company.

Bright shines the sun on creatures mortal;
Men of their neighbors become sensible:
In solitude, for company.

The crow of the cock commands awaking;
Already the mass-bell goes dong-ding:
In solitude, for company.

Men of their neighbors becomes sensible;
God bless the Realm, God bless the People:
In solitude, for company.

Already the mass-bell goes dong-ding;
The dripping mill-wheel is again turning:
In solitude, for company.

God bless the Realm, God bless the People;
God bless this green world temporal:
In solitude, for company.

The dripping mill-wheel is again turning;
Among the leaves the small birds sing:
In solitude, for company.